Mental Maths Ages 1

Anita Straker

![Cambridge University Press logo] **CAMBRIDGE** UNIVERSITY PRESS

1a

1. $100 - 26$.
2. Seven sixes.
3. Treble 5.
4. 35×2.
5. $27 + 43$.
6. How many metres is 321 cm?
7. $9 \div 2$.
8. $\square \times 4 = 44$.
9. Add 3, 8 and 5.
10. Approximately, what is 21×19?

1b

1. Add the odd numbers between 8 and 14.
2. Does my car hold 40 litres or 40 millilitres of petrol in its tank?
3. Write **two thousand and seventeen** in figures.
4. Lucy and Ben shared 12p and 18p equally between them. How much did each of them get?

5. The bus had 32 people on it. 8 got off and 9 got on. How many were on the bus then?

6. What number divided by 7 gives 7?
7. 4 toffees cost 20p. How much are 12 toffees?
8. What is twice the sum of 7 and 15?
9. I have seven 5p coins. If I spend 22p, how much is left?
10. How many triangles can you see altogether ?

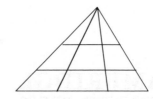

Copy the diagram.

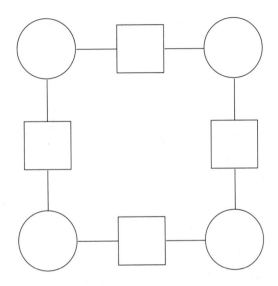

Use each of the numbers 1 to 8.
Write one number in every square and circle.

A number in a square must equal the sum of the two numbers
on each side of it.

1 2 3 4 5 6 7 8

1	72 – 44.	**6**	How many pence is £7.58?
2	10 ÷ 4.	**7**	300 – 250.
3	Double 29.	**8**	Add 4, 9 and 7.
4	9 × 5 + 4.	**9**	7 × 9.
5	38 + 55.	**10**	90 ÷ 3.

2a

1. 20 bottles fill a crate.
   How many full crates will 90 bottles make?

2. If 5 choc-bars cost 15p, what will 20 cost?

3. It is 240 km from here to Nottingham.
   How far is it there and back?

4. Does my new baby sister weigh
   3 kg, 30 kg or 300 g?

5. What is the average of 3, 10 and 5?

6. If $9 \times 17 = 153$, what is 9×18?

7. Put in order, smallest first: 0.9, 1.3, 0.27.

8. Which area is less: a page of this book or $100 \, cm^2$?

9. Approximately, what is double 159?

10. Egg boxes hold a dozen eggs.
    How many boxes are needed for 50 eggs?

2b

1. Seven squared.

2. 48×2.

3. $71 - 34$.

4. $17 \div 2$.

5. $46 + 18$.

6. Nine eights.

7. How many 50p coins make £7.50?

8. $42 \div \square = 6$.

9. $11 \times 5 + 2$.

10. One third of 69.

2c

1. 27 + 29.
2. 36 ÷ 3.
3. 5 × □ = 40.
4. 84 − 38.
5. Half of 72.
6. Twice twenty-five.
7. Add 6, 9 and 3.
8. 21 ÷ 4.
9. How many 20p coins make £3.
10. How many days is 8 weeks?

2d

Stamp card

This card has squares for nine stamps.

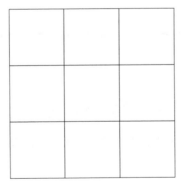

Imagine you have plenty of 1p, 2p, 3p, 4p and 5p stamps.

Each horizontal, vertical or diagonal line of three squares must have three different stamps.

What is the greatest value you can put on the card?

Copy the diagram and show how you could do it.

3a

1. Add 5 to 13 minus 9.
2. Buns are 10 for £1. What do 6 buns cost?
3. It is Thursday, 3rd April. What date was last Sunday?
4. How many hundreds make 8000?
5. A rectangle is 6 cm by 4 cm. What is its area?

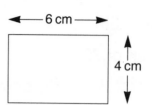

6. If $15 \times 6 = 90$, what is 15×12?
7. It is 19:00 hours. What time was it 40 minutes ago?
8. Find the cost of 20 chews at 5 for 4p.
9. How much longer is 25 days than 2 weeks?
10. What is the change from £1 for 8 crayons at 5p each?

3b

You have two 35p and two 20p stamps.

If you send a parcel using one or more of your stamps, what might it cost?

Write the cost of each possible parcel, starting with the cheapest.

3c

1 What is the angle between 5 and 8 on a clock-face?

2 The perimeter of a square is 8 metres. What is the length of one edge?

3 What number is half way between 32 and 40?

4 If $8 \times 25 = 200$, what is 16×25?

5 Round 4.3 to the nearest whole number.

6 What is the cost of 20 compact discs at £6 each.

7 I use 42 litres of petrol each week. How much is that each day?

8 How many tens make 3000?

9 How many kilograms is 750g?

10 Each small square is 1cm × 1cm. What is the area of the shaded triangle?

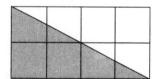

3d

1 Eight sevens.

2 $51 - 35$.

3 Add 7, 9, 2 and 4.

4 $33 \div 4$.

5 $\square \times 5 = 55$.

6 $34 + 47$.

7 Roughly, what is 197×3?

8 $74 \div 2$.

9 How many sixes make 54?

10 315×10.

4a

1	Double 58.	**6**	500×10.
2	$3 \times \square + 1 = 28$.	**7**	$62 - 25$.
3	Nine tenths of £1.	**8**	What is next: 8, 16, 24, 32 …?
4	$79 + 12$.	**9**	$26 \div 2$.
5	$29 \div 4$.	**10**	One third of 24.

4b

Imagine linking four numbers on this grid and adding them together.

The links can go up or down or sideways, but not diagonally.

What is the greatest total you can make?

What is the smallest total you can make?

9	1	6	5
8	3	9	4
5	7	3	8
2	9	7	6

What if the links can only go diagonally?

4c

1	$36 \div 6$.	**6**	Five nines.
2	$47 + 25$.	**7**	Write **one million** in figures.
3	$2 \times 4 \times 4$.	**8**	Divide 38 by 2.
4	Subtract 46 from 93.	**9**	$12 \times \square = 0$.
5	74×100.	**10**	Half of one quarter.

Crack the code

D I N O S A U R

2 3 4 5 6 7 8 9

Multiply together the numbers standing for the letters.

1   Dinosaurs were a lot bigger than **us**. What value has **us**?

2   Which is greater: **do** or **in**?

3   Which is less: **on** or **is**?

4   Find the total of the values of **no** and **or**.

5   Which is the greatest: **an**, **so** or **as**?

6   Work out the value of **and**.

7   Dinosaurs **did odd** things.
     Find the difference in the values of **did** and **odd**.

8   Dinosaurs could **nod**. What is the value of **nod**?

9   Dinosaurs made a **din**. What value has **din**?

10 Dinosaurs slept at **noon**. Find the product for **noon**.

5a

1	Eleven tens.	**6**	Divide 52 by 2.
2	65×100.	**7**	How many twelves make 48?
3	$83 - 45$.	**8**	Add 5, 6 and 7.
4	$48 \div 4$.	**9**	$\square \times 11 = 99$.
5	Increase 66 by 9.	**10**	How many is $1\frac{1}{2}$ dozen?

5b

1 I have nine 5p coins. If I spend 28p, how much will I have left?

2 What is the perimeter of a 4 m by 1 m rectangle?

3 What is this shape called?

4 How many eighths equal three quarters?

5 If I double a number, then subtract 5, the answer is 7. What is the number?

6 Round 8.6 to the nearest whole number.

7 Find the cost of 9 books at £6 each.

8 By how much is 800 ml short of 1 litre?

9 Approximately, what is 58×11?

10 How many degrees clockwise must the pointer turn from 'wash' to 'spin'?

Magic squares

In a magic square the numbers in each row, column and diagonal add up to the same total.

Copy and complete these magic squares.

a.

20		
3	11	
		2

b.

1	15	14	
		7	
8			
13	3	2	16

5d

1   86 − 27.

2   24 ÷ 6.

3   40 × 100.

4   Half of 58.

5   43 + 28.

6   Nine squared.

7   20 − 17 + 13.

8   Add 7, 8 and 9.

9   84 ÷ 4.

10   How many elevens make 77?

6a

1 A pencil costs 9p, and a crayon costs 7p.
   What do 2 pencils and 3 crayons cost?

2 How many days from June 25th to July 2nd?

3 What is the perimeter of a hexagon if one edge is 5 m?

4 Julie spent £3.72. What change did she get from £5?

5 Make the largest number
   you can with these digits.

6 If today is Sunday, what day will it be 30 days from now?

7 Write in figures **ten thousand and twenty-seven**.

8 Tim is 1.32m tall. He is 8cm shorter than Simon.
   How tall is Simon?

9 One factor of 91 is 13. What is the other?

10 What percentage of this circle is shaded?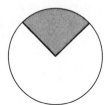

6b

1 $59 + 22$.

2 Nine sevens.

3 $\square \times 6 = 48$.

4 Roughly, what is $496 \div 5$?

5 $5 + 10 + 7 + 2$.

6 $94 - 76$.

7 $60 \div 5$.

8 What is 350 pence in pounds?

9 What is next: 27, 20, 13, 6 …?

10 Find the sum of 17 and 27.

Definitely no magic!

Copy the grid.

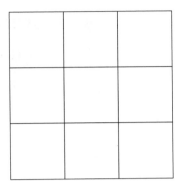

Use each of the numbers 1 to 9.
Write one number in every box.

Each line of three numbers in any direction
must have a **different** total.

Investigate different ways of doing it.

1 2 3 4 5 6 7 8 9

6d

1	45 + 26.	**6**	67 − 38.
2	100 ÷ 5.	**7**	What is 700 millilitres in litres?
3	Add 8, 6 and 9.	**8**	What is next: 8, 17, 26, 35 …?
4	Double 108.	**9**	$6 \times \square = 66$.
5	8 + 9 − 7.	**10**	How many pence in £5.50?

7a

1 Divide 2000 by 20.

2 97 − 29.

3 Three nines.

4 95 ÷ 5.

5 38 + 33.

6 What is the value of 5 in 8.54?

7 How many centimetres in 1.43m?

8 Find the average of 30 and 50.

9 13 + 6 + 3.

10 Find the product of 7, 6 and 2.

7b

1 A coffee costs 20p and a biscuit costs 15p.
   How much is 3 coffees and 2 biscuits?

2 If 27 × 8 = 216, what is 26 × 8?

3 8 golf balls fit in a box.
   How many boxes are needed for 20 golf balls?

4 Put in order, largest first: 0.16, 0.61, 1.6.

5 The small cubes are 1cm × 1cm × 1cm.
   What is the volume of this cuboid?

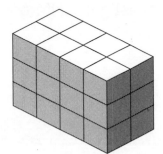

6 A plane goes 48km in 6 minutes.
   How far does it go in 1 minute?

7 Approximately, what is 349 + 122?

8 How many degrees is one sixth of a whole turn?

9 30% of a pattern is red. What percentage is not red?

10 How many triangles
    can you see altogether?

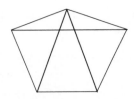

1   71 – 37.

2   Add 10 to 498.

3   70 ÷ 5.

4   Decrease 45 by 19.

5   29 + 46.

6   16 + □ + 5 = 27.

7   Five less than 600.

8   What is 1.56 m in millimetres?

9   14 plus 28.

10   How many quarters in 3.75?

Secret code

Each letter A to F stands for one of these digits.

1 3 4 6 8 9

These sums are in code.

$$A + A = B \qquad A \times A = DF$$

$$C + C = DB \qquad C \times C = BD$$

$$A + C = DE \qquad A \times C = EF$$

Work out what each letter stands for.

Now work out the code answers to these.

a.   E + F.

b.   F + B.

c.   E × F.

d.   F × B.

8a

1. What is the area of a 5 cm by 7 cm rectangle?
2. Write in figures **three million, four thousand and seven**.
3. How many marbles are needed to give 6 children 9 each?
4. How many days is 9 weeks?
5. What is this shape called?

6. How many sixths equal one third?
7. Which area is less: the palm of your hand or 25 cm²?
8. Approximately, what is half of 792?
9. What must be added to 15 to make 39?
10. Find the cost of 6 tubes of sweets, if 2 tubes cost 15p.

8b

Two burglars have six bags of loot and two suitcases.

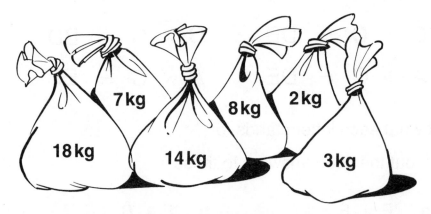

They want to share the load equally between them.

How should they pack their two suitcases?

Mental Maths Ages 10–11 Answers

This book covers:
- addition and subtraction of pairs of large numbers
- tables to 10 x 10
- multiplication and division by 10, 100 and 1000
- fractions and percentages
- mm, cm, m, g, kg, ml, litres
- areas, volumes and perimeters

Task 1a
1 74
2 42
3 15
4 70
5 70
6 3.21 metres
7 4.5 or $4^1/2$
8 11
9 16
10 400

Task 1b
1 33
2 40 litres
3 2017
4 15p
5 33 people
6 49
7 60p
8 44
9 13p
10 18 triangles

Task 1c
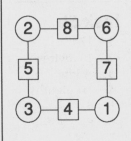

Task 1d
1 28
2 2.5 or $2^1/2$
3 58
4 49
5 93
6 758 pence
7 50
8 20
9 63
10 30

Task 2a
1 4 full crates
2 60p
3 480km
4 3kg
5 6
6 162
7 0.27, 0.9, 1.3
8 100cm²
9 320
10 5 boxes

Task 2b
1 49
2 96
3 37
4 8.5 or $8^1/2$
5 64
6 72
7 15 coins
8 7
9 57
10 23

Task 2c
1 56
2 12
3 8
4 46
5 36
6 50
7 18
8 5.25 or $5^1/4$
9 15 coins
10 56 days

Task 2d
Greatest value is 33p. One solution is this.

5p	4p	2p
4p	1p	5p
3p	5p	4p

Task 3a
1 9
2 60p
3 30th March
4 80
5 24 cm²
6 180
7 18:20 hours
8 16p
9 11 days
10 60p

Task 3b
20p
35p
40p
55p
70p
75p
90p
£1.10

Task 3c
1 90° (270°)
2 2 metres
3 36
4 400
5 4
6 £120
7 6 litres
8 300
9 0.75 kg
10 4 cm²

Task 3d
1 56
2 16
3 22
4 8.25 or $8^1/4$
5 11
6 81
7 600
8 37
9 9
10 3150

Task 4a
1. 116
2. 9
3. 90p
4. 91
5. 7.25 or 7¼
6. 5000
7. 37
8. 40
9. 13
10. 8

Task 4b
Greatest total:
$9 + 7 + 6 + 8 = 30$
Smallest total:
$1 + 3 + 7 + 3 = 14$

With diagonal links
Greatest total:
$8 + 7 + 9 + 8 = 32$
Smallest total:
$5 + 3 + 3 + 4 = 15$

Task 4c
1. 6
2. 72
3. 32
4. 47
5. 7400
6. 45
7. 1 000 000
8. 19
9. 0
10. One eighth ($\frac{1}{8}$)

Task 4d
1. 48
2. in
3. is
4. 65
5. as
6. 56
7. 8
8. 40
9. 24
10. 400

Task 5a
1. 110
2. 6500
3. 38
4. 12
5. 75
6. 26
7. 4
8. 18
9. 9
10. 18

Task 5b
1. 17p
2. 10 metres
3. A kite
4. Six eighths
5. 6
6. 9
7. £54
8. 200 ml
9. 600
10. 120°

Task 5c
a.

20	1	12
3	11	19
10	21	2

b.

1	15	14	4
12	6	7	9
8	10	11	5
13	3	2	16

Task 5d
1. 59
2. 4
3. 4000
4. 29
5. 71
6. 81
7. 16
8. 24
9. 21
10. 7

Task 6a
1. 39p
2. 7 days
3. 30 metres
4. £1.28
5. 43 210
6. Tuesday
7. 10027
8. 1.4 metres
9. 7
10. 25%

Task 6b
1. 81
2. 63
3. 8
4. 100
5. 24
6. 18
7. 12
8. £3.50
9. −1
10. 44

Task 6c
Two solutions are:

1	6	7
8	9	4
3	2	5

1	2	3
8	9	4
7	6	5

Task 6d
1. 71
2. 20
3. 23
4. 216
5. 10
6. 29
7. 0.7 litres
8. 44
9. 11
10. 550 pence.

Task 7a
1. 100
2. 68
3. 27
4. 19
5. 71
6. Five tenths
7. 143 cm
8. 40
9. 22
10. 84

Task 7b
1. 90p
2. 208
3. 3 boxes
4. 1.6, 0.61, 0.16
5. 24 cm³
6. 8 km
7. 470 (or 475)
8. 60°
9. 70%
10. 11 triangles

Task 7c
1. 34
2. 508
3. 14
4. 26
5. 75
6. 6
7. 595
8. 1560 mm
9. 42
10. 15 quarters

Task 7d

A	B	C	D	E	F
4	8	9	1	3	6

a. $E + F = C$
b. $F + B = DA$
c. $E \times F = DB$
d. $F \times B = AB$

Task 8a

1. 35 cm²
2. 3 004 007
3. 54 marbles
4. 63 days
5. A trapezium
6. Two sixths
7. 25 cm²
8. 400
9. 24
10. 45p

Task 8b

Put 26 kg in each suitcase.

18 kg and 8 kg in one suitcase.

3 kg, 14 kg, 7 kg and 2 kg in the other suitcase.

Task 8c

1. 30°
2. 100
3. 44p
4. 50%
5. 45 seconds
6. 103 060
7. 15 °C
8. 5 crates
9. 25 cm
10. 6 paths

Task 8d

1. 27
2. 3
3. 8
4. 48
5. 84
6. 100
7. 5500 ml
8. 27
9. 300
10. 3 hundredths

Task 9a

1. 37p
2. 66p
3. 48p
4. 35p
5. 20p
6. 58p
7. £1.80
8. £2.20
9. 18p
10. £3.30

Task 9b

a.
$$\begin{array}{r} 46 \\ +\ 28 \\ \hline 74 \end{array}$$

b.
$$\begin{array}{r} 38 \\ -\ 29 \\ \hline 9 \end{array}$$

c.
$$\begin{array}{r} 33 \\ +\ 87 \\ \hline 120 \end{array}$$

Task 9c

1. 30 cm
2. 42 millimetres
3. 40%
4. 9
5. 7
6. 20 pens
7. £2.74
8. 13
9. 1 500 000
10. 75 bottles

Task 9d

1. 246
2. 16
3. 64
4. 34
5. 29
6. 85
7. 3600 metres
8. 496
9. 4050
10. No

Task 10a

1. 3.4 or 3²/₅
2. 43
3. £0.60 or 60p
4. 83
5. 39
6. 6068
7. 50
8. 1800 grams
9. One eighth
10. 3 thousandths

Task 10b

1. £4.07
2. 1.1 metres
3. Four sixths
4. 36, 43
5. Parallelogram
6. No
7. 23
8. 1936
9. 8 boxes
10. 11 cm² or 12 cm²

Task 10c

Task 10d

1. 91
2. 56
3. 4.2 or 4¹/₅
4. 27
5. 50
6. 241
7. 300 cm
8. 5903
9. 65
10. 300 (or 270)

Task 11a

1. 120°
2. 5
3. 35 miles
4. 1.6 metres
5. 1000
6. £5000
7. 12 ribbons
8. £1.32
9. 6 km
10. A sphere

Task 11b

1. 27
2. 51
3. 5.4 or 5²/₅
4. 13
5. 0.65 litres
6. 20 millimetres
7. 0.125
8. 112
9. 3 dozen
10. 207

Task 11c

1. 72
2. 76
3. 10000
4. 69
5. 6.6 or 6³/₅
6. 126
7. 0.85 kg
8. 26
9. 2
10. 2500

Task 11d

Total	200	50
Red	28	7
Yellow	56	14
Pink	44	11
Purple	52	13
White	20	5

Task 12a

1 A and D (27)

2 A and E (9)

3 B and C (32)

4 B and E (81)

5 A and C (0.7)

Task 12b

×	4	8	3	5	6
7	28	56	21	35	42
2	8	16	6	10	12
5	20	40	15	25	30
9	36	72	27	45	54

Task 12c

1   13°C
2   288
3   75p
4   32, 76, 130
5   1 (or 1.0)
6   a. 140 b. 235
7   £9.06
8   0.375
9   Cylinder
10 30

Task 12d

1   236
2   110
3   18
4   32
5   23
6   141
7   3 (or 3.0)
8   9
9   1800
10 1, 2, 3, 4, 6, 12

Task 13a

1   33 and 17
2   25 and 13
3   17 and 18
4   18 and 33
5   34 (d17)
6   13 and 28
7   a. 48 b. 86
8   28
9   d13 and d17
10 17 and 33

Task 13b

1   1990
2   46
3   54
4   136
5   32
6   7
7   26
8   0.025 litres
9   42
10 6400

Task 13c

¹1	6	²1
³1	2	1
5	⁴2	7

Task 13d

1   8.4
2   143
3   4007
4   126
5   52
6   75 coins
7   67
8   0.036 kg
9   33
10 48 months

Task 14a

1   153
2   54
3   16
4   23
5   15
6   425
7   10.8 or $10\frac{4}{5}$
8   0.075 km
9   One eighth ($\frac{1}{8}$)
10 99

Task 14b

1   £2.73
2   8 ounces
3   £10
4   Cone
5   4.3
6   0.45 metres
7   70
8   2000
9   304
10 a. 700 b. 350

Task 14c

For example,

182	236	519
493	745	327
675	981	846

Other solutions are possible.

Task 14d

1   41
2   15
3   24
4   Yes
5   144
6   Four eighths
7   77
8   0.085 metres
9   49
10 60

Task 15a

1   26
2   9.8 or $9\frac{4}{5}$
3   36
4   10000
5   143
6   16 ounces
7   9
8   0.1 kg
9   20
10 No

Task 15b

1   210°
2   20p (£0.20)
3   1000 miles
4   180
5   6 ways
6   8p
7   57, 59, 61
8   207015
9   21
10 6 and 6

Task 15c

1   125
2   35
3   36
4   183
5   400
6   34
7   0.05 km
8   16
9   2100
10 8 pints

Task 15d

T   R   I   C   K
12 14 11 8   10

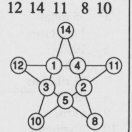

8c

1. What is the **acute** angle between the hands at 1 o'clock?

2. How many hundreds in 10 000?

3. What is the change from £1 for two cakes at 28p each?

4. 43 of the 86 books on a shelf are paperbacks. What percentage is this?

5. How many seconds in three quarters of a minute?

6. Write in figures **one hundred and three thousand and sixty**.

7. If the temperature rose by 18° from −3 °C, what would it be?

8. A crate holds 25 bottles. How many crates will hold 106 bottles?

9. The perimeter of a square is 100 cm. What is the length of one edge?

10. Moves along the lines can be to the right or down. How many different paths from A to B are there?

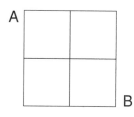

8d

1. 46 − 19.

2. 75 ÷ 25.

3. Two cubed.

4. Eight sixes.

5. 67 + 17.

6. Roughly, what is 398 ÷ 4?.

7. What is 5.5 litres in millilitres?

8. 15 + 8 + 4.

9. 6000 ÷ 20.

10. What is the value of 3 in 2.73?

Shopping

Anna bought these.

Colin bought these.

Sharon bought these.

+01	00.66+
+01	00.55+
+01	00.76+
+01	00.35+
+01	00.64+
+01	00.64+
+01	00.37+

+01	00.76+
+01	00.35+
+01	00.64+
+01	00.60+
+01	00.60+
+01	00.20+
+01	00.48+

+01	00.37+
+01	00.37+
+01	00.60+
+01	00.35+
+01	00.55+
+01	00.48+
+01	00.58+

Use the till receipts to work out the prices of these.

1 A tin of beans.   **3** A tin of soup.   **5** An orange.

2 Ketchup.   **4** A bottle of milk.   **6** A packet of rice.

7 What would 3 boxes of eggs cost?

8 What would 4 packets of tea cost?

9 How much more is the cereal than the rice?

10 What was the total cost of Sharon's purchases?

9b

Copy and complete these sums.

a.
$$\begin{array}{r} 4\ \square \\ +\ \square\ 8 \\ \hline 7\ 4 \end{array}$$

b.
$$\begin{array}{r} 3\ \square \\ -\ \square\ 9 \\ \hline 9 \end{array}$$

c.
$$\begin{array}{r} 3\ \square \\ +\ \square\ 7 \\ \hline \square\ 2\ 0 \end{array}$$

9c

1 Find the perimeter of a 9 cm by 6 cm rectangle.

2 How many mm in 4.2 cm?

3 What percentage of the rectangle is shaded?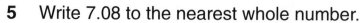

4 If 342 = 38 × 9, what is 342 ÷ 38?

5 Write 7.08 to the nearest whole number.

6 A pen is 15p. How many do you get for £3?

7 I spent £7.26. What was my change from £10?

8 Double a number is 4 less than 30. What is it?

9 Write in figures **one and a half million**.

10 If 30 bottles fill a crate, how many bottles in 2½ crates?

9d

1 Double 123.

2 80 ÷ 5.

3 Square 8.

4 62 − 28.

5 13 + 9 + 7.

6 48 + 37.

7 How many metres in 3.6 km?

8 Subtract 10 from 506.

9 Multiply 405 by 10.

10 Is 38 a multiple of 4?

10a

1	$17 \div 5$.	**6**	Add 100 to 5968.
2	$81 - 38$.	**7**	Roughly, what is $503 \div 11$?
3	Three fifths of £1.	**8**	How many grams in 1.8 kg?
4	29 plus 54.	**9**	What fraction of £2 is 25p?
5	$13 + 21 + 5$.	**10**	What is the value of 3 in 0.073?

10b

1 Andrew has spent half his savings of £8.14.
How much has he left?

2 Add half a metre to 60 centimetres.

3 How many sixths equal two thirds?

4 What two numbers come next: 1, 8, 15, 22, 29 …?

5 What is this shape called?

6 A bottle of lemonade costs 35p.
Can you buy three bottles with £1?

7 What is the next prime number after 19?

8 Grandad was 15 in 1951. When was he born?

9 60 tea-bags fill a box.
How many boxes can be filled with 500 tea-bags?

10 The small squares are 1cm by 1cm.
What is the approximate area
of the oval?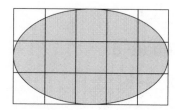

Mystery product

Copy and complete this multiplication .

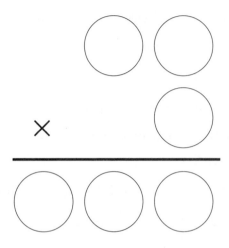

Use each of the numbers 1 to 6.

Write one number in every circle to make the answer correct.

1 2 3 4 5 6

1	65 + 26.	**6**	Half of 482.
2	Seven eights.	**7**	What is 3m in centimetres?
3	21 ÷ 5.	**8**	6003 minus 100.
4	84 – 57.	**9**	Multiply 13 by 5.
5	18 + 32.	**10**	Approximately, what is 32 × 9?

11a

1   What is the **obtuse** angle between
    1 and 5 on a clock-face?

2   One factor of 85 is 17. What is the other?

3   8 km is about 5 miles. About how many miles is 56 km?

4   If 40 cm is cut from a 2 m plank, how much is left?

5   How many thousands make one million?

6   A company director earning £50 000 had a 10% pay rise.
    How much extra did she earn?

7   How many 25 cm ribbons can be cut from 3 metres of ribbon?

8   What is the cost of 6 tubes of sweets at 22p each?

9   A plane goes 54 km in 9 minutes.
    How far does it go in 1 minute?

10 What shape do you get if you rotate
    a circle about its diameter?

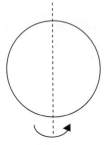

11b

1   Three cubed.

2   13 + 20 + 18.

3   27 ÷ 5.

4   82 − 69.

5   What is 650 ml in litres?

6   How many millimetres is 2 cm?

7   Write **one eighth** as a decimal.

8   48 + 64.

9   How many dozen is 36?

10 $23 \times 18 = 414$. What is 23×9?

1	Eight nines.	**6**	Increase 68 by 58.
2	40 + 20 + 16.	**7**	How many kilograms is 850 g?
3	100 squared.	**8**	5 + 9 + 4 + 8.
4	98 − 29.	**9**	One twelfth of 24.
5	33 ÷ 5.	**10**	Roughly, what is 55 × 45?

Sweet peas

The graph shows as percentages the colours of sweet peas in a large bowl of flowers.

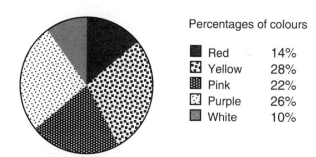

Percentages of colours

■	Red	14%
▨	Yellow	28%
▦	Pink	22%
▢	Purple	26%
▨	White	10%

How many of each colour are there in bowls of 200 and 50 flowers? Copy and complete the table.

Total no. of flowers	200	50
Red		
Yellow		
Pink		
Purple		
White		

In each row, find the two sums with the same answer.

	A	B	C	D	E
1	$51 - 24$	$36 \div 3$	$10 + 16$	3×9	Half of 50
2	$36 \div 4$	2×7	$42 \div 6$	Half of 16	3^2
3	5×7	$64 \div 2$	$2^3 \times 4$	$14 + 17$	4×9
4	$35 + 47$	9^2	$161 \div 2$	$65 + 15$	$100 - 19$
5	$2.1 \div 3$	4×0.2	$0.5 + 0.2$	$1 - 0.4$	0.25×3

12b

Copy and complete this multiplication table.

$\times$		8	3		6
	28			35	
2			6		
	20		15		
					54

1   At noon the temperature was 8°C.
By midnight it was –5°C.
What was the drop in temperature?

2   If 15 × 18 = 270, what is 16 × 18?

3   How much is it for fifteen 5p stamps?

4   If each number is the sum of the two previous numbers,
what are the missing numbers in this pattern?

□, 22, 54, □, □.

5   What is next: 0.2, 0.4, 0.6, 0.8 …?

6   To multiply by 5, multiply by 10 and halve. What is:

    a.   28 × 5   **b.**   47 × 5?

7   Double £4.53.

9   Write **three eighths** as a decimal.

8   What shape do you get if you
rotate a square about an edge?

10   Approximately, what is 593 ÷ 20?

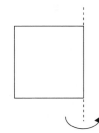

1   Half of 472.

2   20 + 30 + 60.

3   54 – 36.

4   96 ÷ 3.

5   3 + 7 + 8 + 5.

6   87 + 54.

7   Add one tenth to 2.9.

8   9 + □ + 8 = 26.

9   Multiply 9 by 200.

10   What are the factors of 12?

Darts

Darts landing in the shaded area score double.

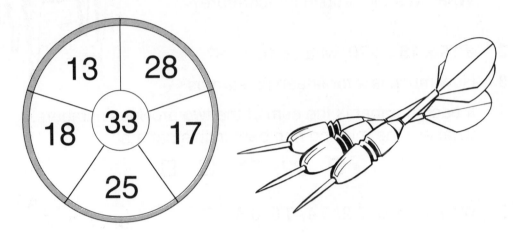

1 Which two numbers have a difference of 16?

2 Which two have a difference of 12?

3 Karen scored 35 with two darts. What did she hit?

4 Dean scored 51 with two darts. What were the numbers?

5 Karen's double was 8 more than Dean's double.
What was her score?

6 Tracey scored 41. Which two numbers did she land on?

7 If three darts land on different numbers, with no doubles:
   a.   what is the lowest score you can get;
   b.   what is the highest score you can get?

8 Dean got three darts on the same number. His score was 84.
What number did his darts hit?

9 Karen scored two doubles. Her score was 60.
What two doubles did she get?

10 Dean scored a double.
Tracey equalled his score with two darts.
Which two numbers did she land on?

13b

1	10 less than 2000.	**6**	Find the average of 5, 8 and 8.
2	63 – 17.	**7**	4 + 6 + 9 + 7.
3	Nine sixes.	**8**	How many litres is 25 ml?
4	49 + 87.	**9**	Find the product of 2, 3 and 7.
5	128 ÷ 4.	**10**	Roughly, what is 79×81?

13c

Copy and complete this cross-number puzzle.

Across

1. A square number.

3. A square palindromic number.

4. A cube number.

Down

1. 23×5.

2. A multiple of 13.

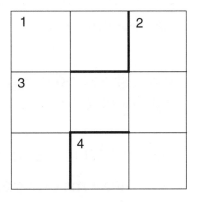

Hint: a palindromic number reads the same forwards as backwards.

13d

1	42 ÷ 5.	**6**	How many 2p coins make £1.50?
2	85 + 58.	**7**	95 – 28.
3	Add 1000 to 3007.	**8**	How many kilograms is 36 g?
4	Double 9 times 7.	**9**	What is next: 47, 45, 42, 38 …?
5	Divide 208 by 4.	**10**	How many months is 4 years?

14a

1	96 + 57.	**6**	Half of 850.
2	$9 \times 3 \times 2$.	**7**	$54 \div 5$.
3	$\square - 9 + 14 = 21$.	**8**	How many kilometres is 75 m?
4	2 + 9 + 7 + 5.	**9**	1 minus $^7/_8$.
5	51 − 36.	**10**	Eleven nines.

14b

1   I spent £12.27. What was my change from £15?

2   25 g is about one ounce. About how many ounces is 200 g?

3   What is 20% of £50?

4   What shape do you get if you rotate a
right-angled triangle about its shortest side?

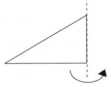

5   Round 4.29 to the nearest tenth.

6   How many **metres** between the arrows?

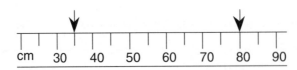

7   Find the average of 35 and 105.

8   Approximately, what is 39×52?

9 $8 \times 19 = 152$. What is 16×19?

10   To multiply by 25, multiply by 100 and divide by 4. What is:

    a. 28×25 **b.** 14×25?

Hundreds, tens and units

Copy this addition sum.

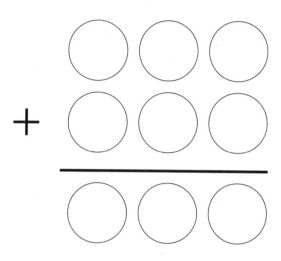

Use each of the numbers 1 to 9.

Write one number in each circle to make the sum correct.

1 2 3 4 5 6 7 8 9

1   164 ÷ 4.

2   42 – 27.

3   8 + 4 + 7 + 5.

4   Is 47 a prime number?

5   68 + 76.

6   How many eighths is one half?

7   What is next: 57, 59, 63, 69 …?

8   How many metres is 85 mm?

9   Find the average of 65 and 33.

10   75% of 80.

15a

1. $6 + 8 + 3 + 5 + 4$.
2. $49 \div 5$.
3. $62 - 26$.
4. 10×1000.
5. $59 + 84$.
6. How many ounces in 1 lb?
7. What is next: 31, 27, 22, 16 …?
8. How many kilograms is 100 g?
9. Roughly, what is $403 \div 19$?
10. Is 50 a multiple of 4?

15b

1. What is the **reflex** angle between 9 and 2 on a clock face?

2. What is 10% of £2?
3. I drive 12000 miles a year. What is my monthly average?
4. If $12 \times 16 = 192$, what is 12×15?
5. How many different ways could you shade two of these four squares?

6. What is the price of one stamp if 1000 cost £80?
7. What are the prime numbers between 55 and 65?
8. Write in figures **two hundred and seven thousand and fifteen**.
9. What is the total number of spots on a 6-sided dice?
10. Two dice are rolled. What numbers are face down if all the spots showing total 30?

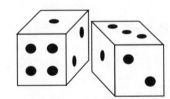

1   25×5.

2   $5 + 6 + 7 + 8 + 9$.

3   $2 \times 3 \times 2 \times 3$.

4   $87 + 96$.

5   Multiply 8 by 50.

6   $63 - 29$.

7   How many kilometres is 50 m?

8   What is next: 42, 37, 31, 24 …?

9   Approximately, what is 31×72?

10 How many pints in a gallon?

Magic star

The numbers along each line of this magic star add up to 28.

The letters **TRICK** stand for 8, 10, 11, 12 and 14.
Which letter is which?

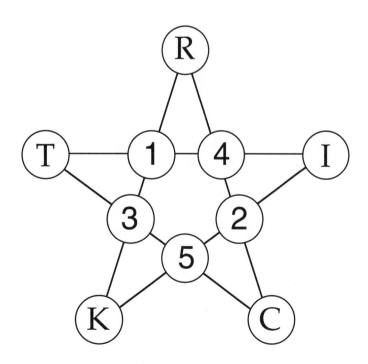

PUBLISHED BY THE PRESS SYNDICATE OF THE UNIVERSITY OF CAMBRIDGE
The Pitt Building, Trumpington Street, Cambridge CB2 1RP, United Kingdom

CAMBRIDGE UNIVERSITY PRESS
The Edinburgh Building, Cambridge CB2 2RU, United Kingdom
40 West 20th Street, New York, NY 10011-4211, USA
10 Stamford Road, Oakleigh, Melbourne 3166, Australia

© Cambridge University Press 1994, 1998

This edition first published 1998

Printed in the United Kingdom by Scotprint Ltd, Musselburgh

A catalogue record for this book is available from the British Library

ISBN 0 521 65559 5 paperback

Cover Illustration by Tony Hall
Cartoons by Tim Sell